Body Coverings

Scales

Cassie Mayer

Heinemann Library
Chicago, Illinois

Customer Service   888–454–2279

Visit our website at www.heinemannlibrary.com

Photo research by Tracy Cummins and Erica Newbery
Designed by Jo Hinton-Malivoire
Printed and bound in China by South China Printing Company
10 09 08
10 9 8 7 6 5 4 3 2

Library of Congress Cataloging-in-Publication Data
Mayer, Cassie.
  Scales / Cassie Mayer.-- 1st ed.
     p. cm. -- (Body coverings)
  Includes bibliographical references and index.
  ISBN 1-4034-8374-4 (hc) -- ISBN 1-4034-8380-9 (pb)
  ISBN 978-1-4034-8374-4 (hc) -- ISBN 978-1-4034-8380-5 (pb)
  1. Scales (Fishes)--Juvenile literature. 2. Scales (Reptiles)--Juvenile literature. I. Title. II. Series.
  QL942.M375 2006
  573.5'95--dc22
                                           2005035408

Acknowledgments
The author and publisher are grateful to the following for permission to reproduce copyright material:
Alamy p. **22** (eagle, Nature Picture Library/Jeff Foott); Corbis pp. **4** (rhino, Royalty Free), **7** and **8** (Joe McDonald), **9** and **10** (scales, Clouds Hill Imaging Ltd.), **10** (shark, Tim Davis), **11** and **12** (Nigel J. Dennis/Gallo Images), **13** (microscopic scales, George D. Lepp and butterfly, Ralph A. Clevenger), **20** (Kevin Dodge); Getty Images pp. **6** (Allofs), **14** (Bumgarner), **15** (Rotman), **16** (Wolcott Henry III), **17** (Wolfe), **18** (Wolfe), **23** (Wolfe); Getty Images/Digital Vision pp. **4** (kingfisher, cheetah); Getty Images/PhotoDisc p. **4** (snail), **5**, **23**; Nature Picture Library p. **22** (turtle, Jeff Rotman); NHPA p. **22** (shark, Doug Perrine).

Cover image of scales reproduced with permission of Strand/Getty Images. Back cover image of snake scales reproduced with permission of Joe McDonald/Corbis.

Special thanks to the Smithsonian Institution and Alfonso Alonso, Gary E. Davis, Helen Ghiradella, Olivier S.G. Pauwels, and Robert Robbins for their help with this project.

Every effort has been made to contact copyright holders of any material reproduced in this book.
Any omissions will be rectified in subsequent printings if notice is given to the publisher.

Contents

feathers

shell

skin

fur

Animals have body coverings.
Body coverings protect animals.

scales

Scales are a body covering.
Scales cover skin.

Many animals have scales.

Scales can be smooth.
What animal is this?

This animal is a snake.
Its scales help it climb.

Scales can be rough.
What animal is this?

This animal is a shark.
Its scales look like small teeth.

Scales can be big.
What animal is this?

This animal is a pangolin.
Its scales are sharp like a knife.

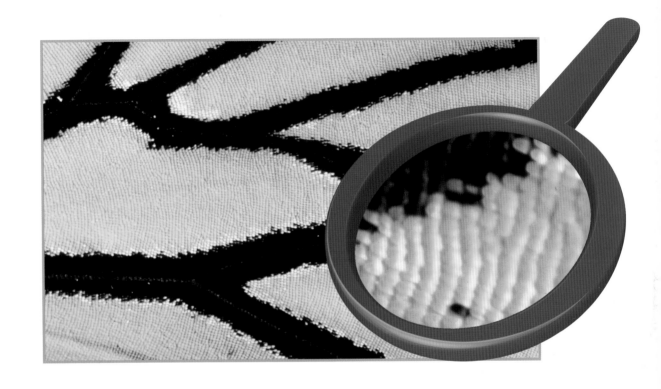

Scales can be small.
What animal is this?

This animal is a butterfly.
Its scales are too small to see.

Scales can be bright colors.
What animal is this?

This animal is a fish.
Its scales feel slimy.

Scales can have patterns.
What animal is this?

This animal is a lizard.
Its scales help it hide.

Do you have scales?

No, you do not have scales!
You have skin.

What if you had scales?
What would your scales be like?

Fun Scale Facts

Bald eagles have scales on their feet.

Turtles have a beak. Their beak is a scale.

Shark teeth are a type of scale.

Picture Glossary

pattern a shape or color that repeats over and over again. Patterns help some animals hide.

scale small plate that covers the body of some animals

Index

Note to Parents and Teachers

In this book, children explore characteristics of scales and are introduced to a variety of animals that use this covering for protection. Visual clues and the repetitive question, "What animal is this?" engage children by providing a predictable structure from which to learn new information. The text has been chosen with the advice of a literacy expert to enable beginning readers success while reading independently or with moderate support. Scientists were consulted to provide both interesting and accurate content.

The book ends with an open-ended question that asks children to relate the material to their lives. Use this question as a writing or discussion prompt to encourage creative thinking and assess comprehension. You can also support children's nonfiction literacy skills by helping them to use the table of contents, picture glossary, and index.